RIS

Rissman, Rebecca.

Shapes in buildings

Spot the Shape

Shapes in Buildings

Rebecca Rissman

Heinemann Library
Chicago, Illinois

© 2009 Heinemann Library
an imprint of Capstone Global Library, LLC
Chicago, Illinois

Customer Service: 888-454-2279

Visit our website at www.heinemannraintree.com

Designed by Joanna Hinton-Malivoire
Photo research by Tracy Cummins and Heather Mauldin
Color Reproduction by Dot Gradations Ltd, UK
Printed and bound by South China Printing Company Ltd

13 12 11 10 09
10 9 8 7 6 5 4 3 2 1

Library of Congress Cataloging-in-Publication Data
Rissman, Rebecca.
Shapes in buildings / Rebecca Rissman.
p. cm. -- (Spot the shape!)
Includes bibliographical references and index.
ISBN 978-1-4329-2172-9 (hc) -- ISBN 978-1-4329-2178-1 (pb) 1. Shapes--Juvenile literature. I. Title.
QA445.5.R5724 2008
516'.15--dc22
                                   2008043210

Acknowledgments
The author and publishers are grateful to the following for permission to reproduce copyright material: ©Age Fotostock pp. **17** (Philip Bier), **18** (Philip Bier); ©Alamy pp. **9** (Robert Harding Picture Library Ltd/Marco Simoni), **10** (Robert Harding Picture Library Ltd/Marco Simoni), **11** (Rainer Jahns), **12** (Rainer Jahns); ©Getty Images pp. **4** (Superstudio), **7** (Keren Su), **8** (Keren Su), **21** (Alan Copson); ©REUTERS pp. **15** (Euroluftbild.de), **16** (Euroluftbild.de), **23b** (Euroluftbild.de); ©Shutterstock pp. **6** (Claudio Zaccherini), **19** (Dainis Derics), **20** (Dainis Derics), **23a** (Dainis Derics); ©Viesti Associates pp. **13** (Ken Ross), **14** (Ken Ross).

Cover photograph of Louvre Museum, Paris reproduced with permission of ©SuperStock/age fotostock. Back cover photograph of a domed building in Cadiz, Spain reproduced with permission of ©Shutterstock (Dainis Derics).

Every effort has been made to contact copyright holders of any material reproduced in this book. Any omissions will be rectified in subsequent printings if notice is given to the publisher.

Contents

Shapes

Shapes are all around us.

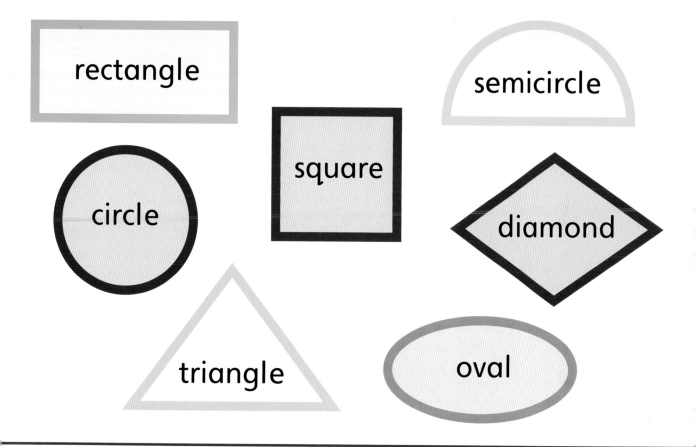

rectangle

semicircle

square

circle

diamond

triangle

oval

Each shape has a name.

Shapes in Buildings

There are many shapes in buildings.

What shape is in this door?

There is a circle in this door.

What shapes are on this building?

This building has diamonds on it.

What shape is in the roofs on
this building?

There are triangles in the roofs on this building.

What shape are these windows?

These windows are squares.

What shape can you see in
this stadium?

There is an oval in this stadium.

What shape is in this house?

A rectangle is in this house.

What shape is the dome on
this building?

The dome is a semicircle.

There are many shapes in buildings.
What shapes can you see?

Naming Shapes

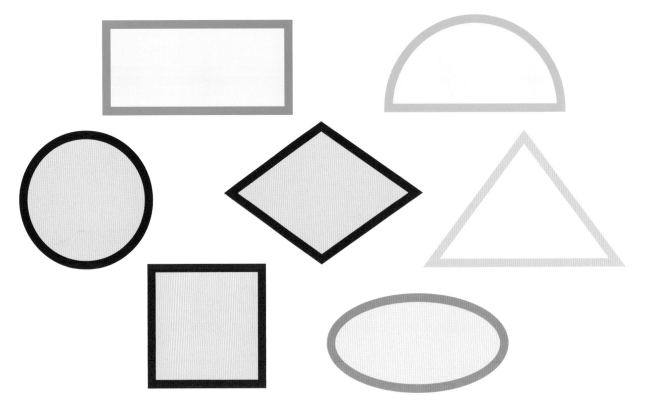

Can you remember the names of these shapes?

Picture Glossary

dome the roof of a building in the shape of the top half of a ball

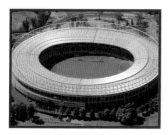

stadium a large building with an area for sports or events with seats for people to sit on

Index

Note to Parents and Teachers

Before reading
Using cardstock, make a set of the shapes shown on page 22. Ask children if they can name the shape. Then ask if they can find examples of that shape in the school building or classroom.

After reading
Make a town skyline with silhouettes of different shapes, for example a steeple, dome, roofs, skyscrapers. Label the buildings and display on the classroom wall. Invite the children to make buildings with different shapes using construction bricks. Ask them to name the shapes they have used.